THE NIGHT FLOWER

For Sonja, William, and Jack

With special thanks to Debbie Colodner, Robin Kropp, and Catherine Bartlett
at the Arizona-Sonora Desert Museum

First U.S. edition 2019
First published in the U.K. in 2018 by Big Picture Press

Library of Congress Catalog Card Number pending
ISBN 978-1-5362-0616-6

18 19 20 21 22 23 TLF 10 9 8 7 6 5 4 3 2 1

Printed in Dongguan, Guangdong, China

This book was typeset in PiS Creatinin Pro.
The illustrations were done in watercolor and colored digitally.

BIG PICTURE PRESS
an imprint of
Candlewick Press
99 Dover Street
Somerville, Massachusetts 02144

www.candlewick.com

THE NIGHT FLOWER

LARA HAWTHORNE

SAGUARO (sa-WAH-ro)

Carnegiea gigantea

The saguaro cactus is found in the Sonoran desert, which stretches
approximately 100,400 square miles/260,000 square kilometers from the
southwestern United States to northwestern Mexico. The saguaro's
flowers are special because they bloom for a single night once a year.
During this short period, their strong scent and brilliant white petals
attract rare pollinators, including bats, moths, and doves.

The desert is greeted by the climbing sun.
It's vibrant and busy now that spring has begun.
Can you spot the saguaros, so spiky and tall?
A haven for wildlife, the large and the small.

Atop the saguaros, at great lofty heights,
birds can sit safely and rest from their flights.
Woodpeckers tap, making holes with their beaks—
little round homes where they can retreat.

The desert blooms pink, orange, yellow, and red
while bees, birds, and butterflies dance overhead.
Bright-colored petals call out to small beasts,
enticing them nearer for nectar-filled feasts.

Hiding in shade beneath sweet-smelling trees,
wandering deer are enjoying the leaves.
Young squirrels leap from thin branches that sway.
They hop and they hide, carefree as they play.

As temperatures rise, the sun bakes the hard ground.
Sleepy eyes close and there's barely a sound.
Spotty-scaled lizards look out at the view,
waiting for nightfall when noise will ensue.

Animals wait for the night flower show,
but for now the whole desert is sleepy and slow.
A tortoise plods by in the heat of the day,
while a rattlesnake rasps as it snoozes away.

The desert wakes up as the temperature cools.
Animals search for the precious first bloom.
They head for a cactus, the tallest in sight,
waiting and watching as day turns to night.

As the darkness sets in, moths stir in delight,
searching for flowers in the cool desert night.
A fierce, furry hunter with sharp, pointed teeth
howls at the sky on its little pink feet.

And high on the cactus, beneath the bright moon,
a tiny green bud is beginning to bloom. . . .

Its white velvet petals unfurl and reach high,
and a thick fruity fragrance fills the night sky.

As more flowers wake in a chorus of scent,
new creatures appear for this special event.
Brown bats with black wings sense something sweet
and gather to sip from this night-blooming treat.

Around the saguaro, in the shining moonlight,
the desert is festive and thriving tonight.
Bobcats chase pack rats, and ringtails climb high
while the blooms rest like stars against the night sky.

At the dawn of the day, with the new rising sun,
the bats hurry home to take care of their young.
For the birds and the bees there are still a few hours
to visit the cactus and sip from its flowers.

The desert will quiet as the day starts anew.
But the busy saguaro has work yet to do.
Its flowers will close and a red fruit will grow . . .

with seeds that will make a new saguaro.

The Saguaro

Although saguaros can reach heights of up to 49 feet/15 meters, they grow very slowly. In fact, it may take up to two hundred years before they fully mature. Saguaros need very particular conditions, so it can be a struggle for them to grow at all. Only one in many millions of seeds will manage to grow to the same size as its parent.

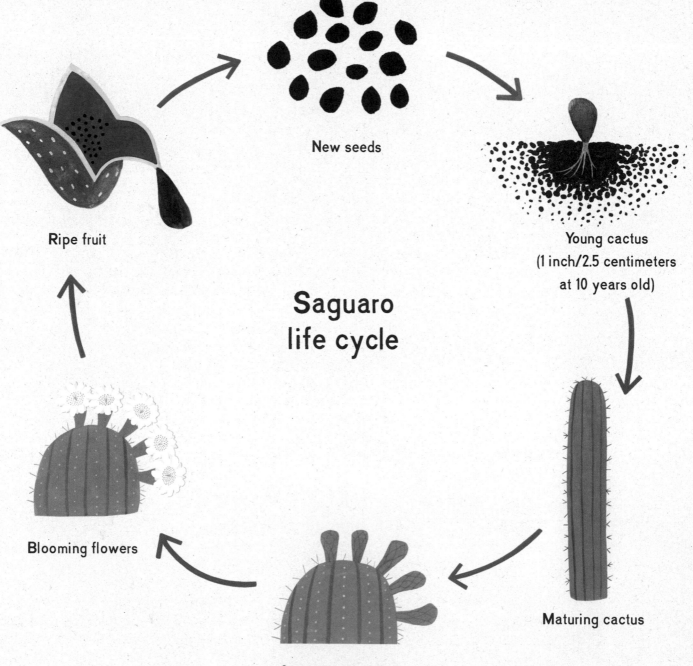

New seeds

Young cactus
(1 inch/2.5 centimeters
at 10 years old)

Saguaro
life cycle

Ripe fruit

Maturing cactus

Blooming flowers

Appearance of buds
(around 35 years old)

CROWN
The flowers and fruit on top of the saguaro are perfectly positioned for flying creatures to feed from.

FRUIT
Each fruit can contain up to 2,000 tiny seeds.

SPINES
Saguaros have spines instead of leaves to protect the precious water inside their trunks from animals.

ARM
The saguaro grows its first arm at around 100 years old.

TRUNK
The spongy insides of the cactus can store up to 240 gallons/900 liters of water.

ROOTS
The saguaro has shallow roots, allowing it to soak up water from the ground's surface.

Did you spot . . . ?

Go back through the book and see if you can spot the saguaro's desert friends.

RAINBOW GRASSHOPPER

(Dactylotum bicolor)

These beautiful insects are also called painted grasshoppers because of their brightly colored shells. These colors warn potential predators not to eat them.

LESSER LONG-NOSED BAT

(Leptonycteris yerbabuenae)

The night flower's nectar provides vital fuel for these bats as they cross the Sonoran desert on their annual migration. Several thousand will descend on the desert, dispersing the flower's pollen and seeds as they feed.

RINGTAIL

(Bassariscus astutus)

Members of the raccoon family, these nocturnal mammals use their huge eyes and ears to track down prey. Their Latin name means "clever little fox."

GRASSHOPPER MOUSE

(Onychomys torridus)

These fierce rodents are known to stand on their hind legs and howl at the night. Grasshopper mice eat all sorts of things, including scorpions and venomous centipedes. They are known to stalk their prey like a cat.

GAMBEL'S QUAIL

(Callipepla gambelii)

These small birds get much of their water by eating foods such as cacti fruits. It is rare to see them fly—they prefer to run.

BOBCAT
(Lynx rufus)

Despite being the most common cat in the Sonoran desert, bobcats are rarely seen. They rest in caves or under low-lying trees and hunt rabbits, lizards, and even small deer for food.

SONORAN DESERT TORTOISE
(Gopherus morafkai)

These slow and sturdy creatures are well suited to the dry, hot desert. They keep cool by hiding under plants or in underground burrows and can survive for a long time without water or food.

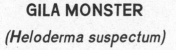

WHITE-LINED SPHINX MOTH
(Hyles lineata)

The Sonoran desert is thriving with moth species. Most only appear at night, when they consume nectar from a variety of sweet-smelling flowers. The white-lined sphinx moth is often compared to a hummingbird because it hovers while it feeds.

GILA MONSTER
(Heloderma suspectum)

These slow-moving reptiles are one of only a few venomous lizards known in the world. They spend much of their time in underground burrows and shelters, and can eat as much as half their body weight in one feeding!

GILA WOODPECKER
(Melanerpes uropygialis)

Distinctly colored with zebralike markings, these birds are permanent Sonoran dwellers. They use their long, pointy beaks to peck holes in saguaros, where they can raise their chicks safely.

Glossary

BUD
A growth on a plant that will develop into a leaf, flower, or shoot

POLLEN
A dusty substance from a plant that can help other plants to grow

DISPERSE
To spread seeds from a plant

POLLINATE
To move pollen from one plant to another

HABITAT
The natural home of an animal or plant

POLLINATOR
An animal that takes pollen from one plant and passes it to another

MATURE
To develop fully into adulthood

PREDATOR
An animal that eats other animals for food

MIGRATION
A seasonal journey an animal makes, usually in search of food, shelter, or a mate

RIPE
When a fruit is ready to eat

NECTAR
The sugary liquid produced by plants to encourage pollination

SCENT
A smell

NOCTURNAL
Active at night

VENOM
A type of poison produced by animals